Financial Freedom Roadmap - Achieving Early Retirement through the FIRE Movement

Alex on Finance, Volume 1

Alex Thompson

Published by Side Hustle Success, 2023.

While every precaution has been taken in the preparation of this book, the publisher assumes no responsibility for errors or omissions, or for damages resulting from the use of the information contained herein.

FINANCIAL FREEDOM ROADMAP - ACHIEVING EARLY RETIREMENT THROUGH THE FIRE MOVEMENT

First edition. July 4, 2023.

ISBN: 979-8223154860

Written by Alex Thompson.

Table of Contents

Chapter 1: Understanding the FIRE Mindset

1.1 The Concept of Financial Independence

Hey there! Welcome to the exciting journey of achieving financial independence and retiring early. In this chapter, we'll dive into the core concept of financial independence and what it truly means for your life.

Financial independence, simply put, refers to a state where you have accumulated enough wealth and passive income to cover your living expenses without relying on a traditional job or a paycheck. It liberates you from the constraints of a nine-to-five grind and offers the freedom to pursue your passions, spend time with loved ones, and live life on your own terms.

To achieve financial independence, it's crucial to determine your "Financial Independence Number" – the amount of money you need to sustain your desired lifestyle without the need for active income. This number varies from person to person based on factors such as living expenses, future goals, and desired retirement age.

However, financial independence is not synonymous with complete retirement. It's about having the choice to continue working if you find fulfillment in it, pursuing entrepreneurial ventures, or dedicating your time to meaningful endeavors that may not generate substantial income.

1.2 The Benefits of Early Retirement

Retiring early, a significant component of the FIRE movement, offers numerous advantages beyond the conventional retirement age. Early retirement allows you to:

1.2.1 Pursue Your Passions: Imagine waking up every day and being able to dedicate your time to activities that truly ignite your passion and bring you joy. Whether it's traveling, volunteering, starting a business, or exploring new hobbies, early retirement opens up a world of possibilities.

1.2.2 Spend Quality Time with Loved Ones: Often, our work commitments limit the time we can spend with family and friends. Early retirement enables you to strengthen your relationships, create lasting memories, and be present for the important milestones in the lives of your loved ones.

1.2.3 Prioritize Personal Growth: With more time on your hands, you can invest in personal growth and continuous learning. Whether it's acquiring new skills, pursuing further education, or engaging in self-improvement activities, early retirement provides the ideal opportunity to expand your horizons.

1.2.4 Enjoy a Stress-Free Lifestyle: Breaking free from the shackles of financial stress and job-related pressures can significantly improve your overall well-being. Early retirement allows you to embrace a more relaxed and balanced lifestyle, reducing the negative impact of stress on your physical and mental health.

1.3 Setting Clear Financial Goals

To embark on the path to financial independence and early retirement, it's essential to establish clear and specific financial goals.

Setting goals helps you maintain focus and motivation throughout your journey.

Start by asking yourself questions like:

- What age would you like to retire?
- What kind of lifestyle do you envision for your retirement?
- How much money do you need to sustain that lifestyle?

Be specific when setting your financial goals. Instead of saying, "I want to be financially independent," try setting a goal like, "I want to achieve financial independence by age 45, with a passive income of $5,000 per month."

1.4 The Importance of Mindset Shift

Achieving financial independence and retiring early require a mindset shift. It involves reevaluating your relationship with money, adopting new habits, and challenging societal norms.

Embrace the following mindset shifts:

1.4.1 Prioritizing Financial Freedom: Make financial independence a priority in your life. Understand that saving and investing today will lead to a more secure and fulfilling future.

1.4.2 Embracing Frugality: Emphasize the importance of frugality and conscious spending. Focus on distinguishing between needs and wants, and find joy in living a simpler, more intentional lifestyle.

1.4.3 Building a Wealth Mindset: Cultivate a mindset of abundance and wealth creation. Believe that you have the potential to achieve your financial goals and overcome any challenges that come your way.

1.4.4 Embracing Continuous Learning: Recognize the value of financial education and commit to ongoing learning. Stay updated with investment strategies, personal finance principles, and other relevant topics to make informed decisions.

1.5 Embracing Self-Discipline and Delayed Gratification

Financial independence and early retirement require self-discipline and the ability to delay gratification. It means making conscious choices today that will benefit your future self.

Developing self-discipline involves:

1.5.1 Creating a Budget: Establish a budget to track your income and expenses, enabling you to allocate funds toward savings and investments consistently.

1.5.2 Resisting Instant Gratification: Avoid impulsive spending and instead focus on long-term goals. Evaluate each purchase based on its alignment with your financial objectives.

1.5.3 Staying Committed to Savings: Regularly contribute to your savings and investment accounts, even during times of temptation or economic uncertainty. Consistency is key to building wealth over time.

By adopting a FIRE mindset, setting clear goals, and embracing self-discipline, you're laying a strong foundation for your journey towards financial independence and retiring early. In the next chapter, we'll delve into mastering personal finance and building a solid financial base. So, let's continue this exciting adventure together!

Chapter 2: Mastering Personal Finance

2.1 Creating an Effective Budget

Welcome to Chapter 2! In this chapter, we'll focus on one of the fundamental pillars of financial independence: creating an effective budget. A budget serves as a roadmap for managing your income, expenses, and savings. It provides a clear picture of where your money is going and helps you make informed financial decisions.

2.1.1 Tracking Expenses and Identifying Areas of Improvement

To create an effective budget, it's essential to track your expenses and identify areas where you can make improvements. By understanding your spending habits, you can make informed decisions about how to allocate your resources. Here's how to get started:

Step 1: Gather Information: Collect all your financial statements, bank statements, credit card bills, and receipts. This will give you a comprehensive overview of your income and expenses.

Step 2: Categorize Expenses: Categorize your expenses into different categories such as housing, transportation, groceries, utilities, entertainment, and so on. This helps you understand where your money is going and identify areas where you can potentially reduce spending.

Step 3: Analyze Spending Patterns: Take a close look at your expenses within each category. Are there any patterns or trends that emerge? Are there any areas where you're overspending or could cut back? Identifying these patterns will help you make more informed choices about your spending habits.

Step 4: Set Realistic Budget Targets: Based on your analysis, set realistic targets for each category of expenses. Determine how much you want to allocate towards savings, debt repayment, and discretionary spending. Be mindful of your financial goals and adjust your budget accordingly.

2.1.2 Budgeting Tools and Techniques

To make budgeting easier and more efficient, you can leverage various tools and techniques. Here are a few options to consider:

1. Spreadsheet Software: Utilize spreadsheet software like Microsoft Excel or Google Sheets to create your budget. These tools offer flexibility and customization options, allowing you to track income, expenses, and savings easily. You can also find pre-designed budget templates online to kick-start your budgeting process.
2. Budgeting Apps: Take advantage of budgeting apps available for smartphones and computers. These apps often sync with your bank accounts and credit cards, automatically categorize expenses, and provide visual representations of your financial data. Popular budgeting apps include Mint, YNAB (You Need a Budget), and Personal Capital.
3. Envelope System: The envelope system involves allocating cash into different envelopes labeled with different expense categories. This method helps you visualize and control your spending. Once an envelope is empty, you cannot spend any more money in that category for the month.
4. 50/30/20 Rule: The 50/30/20 rule suggests allocating 50% of your income to needs (such as rent, groceries,

utilities), 30% to wants (entertainment, dining out, vacations), and 20% to savings and debt repayment. This rule provides a simple guideline for balancing your financial priorities.

Remember, budgeting is a dynamic process that requires regular review and adjustments. As your financial situation evolves, so should your budget. Be flexible and open to refining your budget over time.

2.2 Managing Debt and Optimizing Credit

Welcome to the section on managing debt and optimizing credit! In this section, we'll delve into strategies for reducing debt and building a good credit score, both of which play a crucial role in your journey towards financial independence and early retirement.

2.2.1 Strategies for Debt Reduction

Debt can be a significant obstacle on the path to financial freedom. Here are some strategies to help you effectively manage and reduce your debt:

1. Create a Debt Repayment Plan: Start by organizing your debts, including credit cards, student loans, car loans, and any other outstanding balances. Prioritize them based on interest rates or pay off the smallest debts first (the snowball method) for quick wins and motivation. Allocate a specific amount of money from your budget to debt repayment each month.
2. Cut Expenses and Increase Income: Look for ways to reduce your expenses and increase your income to allocate

more funds towards debt repayment. Consider downsizing your living arrangements, reducing discretionary spending, or taking on a side hustle or freelance work to boost your income.

3. Negotiate with Creditors: If you're struggling to meet your debt obligations, don't hesitate to contact your creditors. They may be willing to negotiate a lower interest rate or develop a repayment plan that better suits your financial situation.
4. Debt Consolidation: Explore options for consolidating high-interest debts into a single, lower-interest loan. This can simplify your repayment process and potentially reduce the total interest you'll pay over time.
5. Seek Professional Help if Needed: If you find yourself overwhelmed by debt, consider reaching out to a credit counseling agency or a financial advisor. They can provide guidance on debt management strategies and help you create a personalized plan to become debt-free.

2.2.2 Building and Maintaining a Good Credit Score

Your credit score plays a significant role in financial matters such as obtaining loans, securing favorable interest rates, and even renting an apartment. Here are some tips to build and maintain a good credit score:

1. Pay Bills on Time: Your payment history is one of the most crucial factors in determining your credit score. Make it a priority to pay your bills, including credit card bills, loans, and utilities, on time. Consider setting up automatic payments or reminders to ensure timely payments.

2. Keep Credit Card Balances Low: Aim to keep your credit card balances well below their limits. High credit utilization can negatively impact your credit score. Ideally, aim to use no more than 30% of your available credit.
3. Avoid Opening Unnecessary Credit Accounts: Each time you apply for credit, a hard inquiry is placed on your credit report, which can temporarily lower your credit score. Only open new accounts when necessary and avoid excessive credit applications.
4. Monitor Your Credit Report: Regularly check your credit report for errors or discrepancies that could negatively impact your credit score. You can obtain a free copy of your credit report from each of the three major credit bureaus once a year at AnnualCreditReport.com.
5. Maintain a Mix of Credit: Having a mix of credit types, such as credit cards, loans, and a mortgage, can positively influence your credit score. However, only take on credit that you genuinely need and can manage responsibly.

Remember, building and maintaining a good credit score is a long-term endeavor. Consistent responsible financial behavior over time will help improve your creditworthiness and open doors to favorable financial opportunities.

2.3 Investing Principles for Long-Term Wealth Accumulation

Welcome to the section on investing principles for long-term wealth accumulation! In this section, we'll explore the key concepts and strategies to help you make informed investment decisions and grow your wealth on the path to financial independence and early retirement.

2.3.1 Understanding Different Investment Options

Investing is an essential component of building long-term wealth. Understanding different investment options will enable you to make informed choices aligned with your financial goals. Here are some common investment options to consider:

1. Stocks: Stocks represent ownership shares in publicly traded companies. Investing in stocks allows you to participate in the company's growth and share in its profits through capital appreciation and dividends.
2. Bonds: Bonds are debt securities issued by governments, municipalities, or corporations. When you invest in bonds, you lend money to the issuer in exchange for regular interest payments and the return of the principal amount at maturity.
3. Mutual Funds: Mutual funds pool money from multiple investors to invest in a diversified portfolio of stocks, bonds, or other assets. They are managed by professional fund managers, offering diversification and convenience for individual investors.
4. Exchange-Traded Funds (ETFs): ETFs are similar to mutual funds but trade on stock exchanges like individual stocks. They offer diversification and flexibility while providing exposure to specific sectors, asset classes, or investment strategies.
5. Real Estate: Investing in real estate involves purchasing properties for rental income or capital appreciation. Real estate can provide steady cash flow and potential tax benefits, but it requires careful research and management.
6. Index Funds: Index funds are a type of mutual fund or

ETF that aims to replicate the performance of a specific market index, such as the S&P 500. They offer broad market exposure and low fees, making them popular among passive investors.

2.3.2 Risk vs. Reward: Assessing Your Risk Tolerance

Investing inherently involves risk, and it's essential to assess your risk tolerance before making investment decisions. Your risk tolerance depends on factors such as your financial goals, time horizon, and comfort level with market fluctuations. Here are some considerations:

1. Time Horizon: Longer investment horizons generally allow for a higher tolerance for short-term market volatility. If you have a long time until retirement, you may be more willing to accept higher-risk investments with potentially higher returns.
2. Financial Goals: Consider your financial goals and the level of risk needed to achieve them. If your goals are more conservative, you may opt for lower-risk investments, whereas more ambitious goals may require a higher level of risk.
3. Risk Capacity: Assess your financial situation, including your income, expenses, and existing assets. Having a solid financial foundation and emergency fund can provide a buffer against potential investment losses.
4. Emotional Resilience: Be honest with yourself about how you handle market fluctuations and uncertainty. If you tend to panic during market downturns, you may prefer a more conservative investment approach.

2.3.3 Building an Investment Portfolio

Building a well-diversified investment portfolio is crucial for managing risk and maximizing returns. Here are some steps to consider when constructing your investment portfolio:

1. Define Your Asset Allocation: Determine the percentage of your portfolio allocated to different asset classes, such as stocks, bonds, and alternative investments. This allocation should align with your risk tolerance and financial goals.
2. Diversify Within Asset Classes: Within each asset class, diversify your holdings to reduce the risk associated with individual investments. For example, in the stock market, diversify across different industries, company sizes, and geographical regions.
3. Regularly Rebalance: Regularly review and rebalance your portfolio to maintain your desired asset allocation. Rebalancing involves selling overperforming assets and buying underperforming ones to maintain your desired balance.
4. Consider Dollar-Cost Averaging: Dollar-cost averaging involves investing a fixed amount of money regularly, regardless of market conditions. This approach can help smooth out the impact of market volatility over time.
5. Stay Informed and Seek Professional Advice: Stay updated on market trends, economic indicators, and investment news. Consider seeking guidance from a financial advisor who can provide personalized advice based on your individual circumstances.

Remember, investing is a long-term endeavor, and patience is key. While the market may experience short-term fluctuations, focus on your long-term financial goals and stay committed to your investment strategy.

Chapter 3: Maximizing Income Generation

3.1 Beyond Traditional Employment

Welcome to Chapter 3! In this chapter, we'll explore strategies for maximizing your income generation beyond traditional employment. By diversifying your income sources, you can accelerate your progress towards financial independence and early retirement.

3.1.1 Exploring Freelancing and Consulting Opportunities

Freelancing and consulting offer flexibility, independence, and the potential for higher income. Here are some steps to explore these opportunities:

1. Identify Your Skills: Assess your skills and expertise that can be valuable to others. Consider your professional experience, hobbies, or specialized knowledge that can be monetized.
2. Define Your Niche: Determine your target market and the specific services you can offer. Having a niche allows you to position yourself as an expert and attract clients who value your unique skills.
3. Build a Professional Network: Leverage your existing network and establish new connections to find potential clients. Attend industry events, join professional associations, and utilize online platforms like LinkedIn to expand your network.
4. Market Your Services: Create a compelling portfolio or website that showcases your skills and previous work.

Utilize social media, online job platforms, and word-of-mouth referrals to market yourself effectively.

5. Provide Outstanding Service: Deliver exceptional work and provide excellent customer service to build a strong reputation. Satisfied clients are more likely to refer you to others and provide testimonials that can attract new clients.

Remember, freelancing and consulting require self-discipline, time management, and the ability to handle client relationships. However, they can offer flexibility, control over your work, and potentially higher earnings.

3.1.2 Building Passive Income Streams

Passive income streams allow you to generate income with minimal active effort. Here are some avenues to consider for building passive income:

1. Rental Properties: Invest in real estate properties that generate rental income. This can include residential properties, commercial spaces, or vacation rentals. Property management companies can handle day-to-day operations if you prefer a more hands-off approach.
2. Dividend-Paying Stocks: Invest in stocks that provide regular dividend payments. Dividends are a portion of a company's profits distributed to shareholders, providing a steady income stream.
3. Peer-to-Peer Lending: Participate in peer-to-peer lending platforms, where you can lend money to individuals or small businesses in exchange for interest payments.

Conduct thorough research and assess the risks associated with each lending opportunity.

4. Royalties and Licensing: If you have creative works, such as books, music, or art, consider earning royalties through licensing agreements. This allows others to use your intellectual property in exchange for recurring payments.
5. Digital Products and Online Courses: Create and sell digital products, such as e-books, online courses, or software applications. Once created, these products can generate passive income as long as there is demand.

Building passive income streams may require upfront investment, time, and effort. However, they have the potential to generate ongoing income and provide financial security in the long run.

3.2 Advancing Your Career

Welcome to the section on advancing your career! In this section, we'll explore strategies for professional growth, skill development, and negotiating higher salaries and benefits. By continuously improving your skills and advocating for yourself, you can enhance your earning potential and accelerate your journey to financial independence and early retirement.

3.2.1 Strategies for Professional Growth and Skill Development

Investing in your professional growth is essential for long-term career success. Here are some strategies to consider:

1. Set Clear Career Goals: Define your career aspirations and set specific, achievable goals. Identify the skills and experiences you need to reach your desired position or

industry.

2. Continuous Learning: Commit to lifelong learning and skill development. Stay updated on industry trends, enroll in relevant courses or certifications, and attend workshops or conferences to enhance your knowledge and expertise.
3. Seek Mentors and Networking Opportunities: Connect with experienced professionals in your field who can offer guidance and support. Attend networking events, join professional organizations, and seek mentorship to gain valuable insights and expand your professional network.
4. Take on Challenging Projects: Volunteer for projects or assignments that push you outside your comfort zone. Embrace new responsibilities and challenges to demonstrate your capabilities and grow your skill set.
5. Develop Soft Skills: In addition to technical skills, focus on developing strong interpersonal and communication skills, leadership abilities, and adaptability. These skills are highly valued in the workplace and can open doors to new opportunities.

Remember, professional growth is a continuous process. Embrace a growth mindset and remain proactive in seeking new learning opportunities throughout your career.

3.2.2 Negotiating Higher Salaries and Benefits

Negotiating your salary and benefits can significantly impact your financial well-being. Here are some tips for successful negotiations:

1. Research Market Rates: Before negotiations, research industry standards and salary ranges for your position. This

knowledge provides leverage and helps you make a compelling case for fair compensation.

2. Highlight Your Value: Clearly articulate the value you bring to the organization. Showcase your accomplishments, skills, and the impact you've made in your current or previous roles. Demonstrate how your contributions have benefited the company's bottom line.
3. Be Confident and Prepared: Enter negotiations with confidence and a well-prepared strategy. Anticipate potential objections or counteroffers and be ready to respond effectively. Practice your negotiation skills beforehand to feel more comfortable during the actual conversation.
4. Consider Total Compensation: Look beyond just the base salary and consider the complete compensation package, including benefits, bonuses, stock options, and retirement plans. Evaluate the overall value and assess how it aligns with your financial goals.
5. Be Open to Non-Monetary Perks: If a salary increase isn't immediately feasible, explore other non-monetary perks that can enhance your overall job satisfaction. This can include flexible work arrangements, professional development opportunities, or additional vacation time.

Remember, negotiation is a two-way process. Aim for a win-win outcome where both parties feel satisfied with the agreement. Be respectful and professional throughout the negotiation process.

3.3 Entrepreneurship and Side Hustles

Welcome to the section on entrepreneurship and side hustles! In this section, we'll explore the world of entrepreneurship, including identifying lucrative business ideas and tips for successfully managing side businesses. By leveraging your skills and entrepreneurial spirit, you can create additional income streams and fast-track your path to financial independence and early retirement.

3.3.1 Identifying Lucrative Business Ideas

Starting a business or pursuing a side hustle can be an exciting and rewarding venture. Here are some steps to help you identify lucrative business ideas:

1. Assess Your Skills and Passions: Consider your skills, expertise, and areas of interest. Identify activities or services that align with your strengths and passions, as this will increase your motivation and chances of success.
2. Research Market Demand: Conduct market research to identify potential gaps or opportunities. Evaluate customer needs, competition, and trends in your target market to ensure there is demand for your product or service.
3. Solve a Problem: Look for problems or pain points that people face and develop a solution. Solving a pressing problem can create a loyal customer base and set your business apart from competitors.
4. Consider Your Resources: Assess the resources available to you, including time, capital, and networks. Choose business ideas that are realistic and feasible given your current circumstances.
5. Test and Validate: Before fully committing, test your business idea on a small scale. Seek feedback, conduct

surveys, or create a minimum viable product (MVP) to gauge market interest and gather valuable insights.

Remember, entrepreneurship requires dedication, perseverance, and adaptability. Be prepared for challenges along the way and embrace a mindset of continuous improvement.

3.3.2 Tips for Successfully Managing Side Businesses

Managing a side business alongside your regular job or other responsibilities requires careful planning and organization. Here are some tips for effectively managing your side hustle:

1. Set Clear Goals and Priorities: Define your goals for the side business and prioritize tasks accordingly. Create a schedule or timeline to ensure you allocate dedicated time for your entrepreneurial endeavors.
2. Time Management: Efficiently manage your time by creating a routine and setting boundaries. Eliminate distractions, delegate tasks where possible, and utilize productivity tools or techniques to maximize your productivity.
3. Delegate and Outsource: As your side business grows, consider delegating tasks or outsourcing certain functions. This can free up your time and allow you to focus on higher-value activities.
4. Build a Support Network: Surround yourself with a supportive network of mentors, fellow entrepreneurs, or business communities. Seek advice, collaborate, and learn from others who have experience in your industry or niche.
5. Separate Finances: Maintain clear separation between your

personal and business finances. Open a separate bank account and track your income and expenses meticulously to ensure accurate financial management.

6. Stay Compliant: Familiarize yourself with the legal and regulatory requirements for your business. Ensure you meet all licensing, tax, and reporting obligations to avoid any legal issues down the road.
7. Continuously Learn and Adapt: Stay updated on industry trends, consumer preferences, and business best practices. Be open to feedback, learn from your experiences, and adapt your strategies as needed to stay competitive.

Managing a side business requires commitment and persistence, but it can be a fulfilling and financially rewarding endeavor. Remember to strike a balance between your side hustle and other aspects of your life to avoid burnout.

Chapter 4: Minimizing Expenses and Lifestyle Optimization

4.1 Embracing Frugality

Welcome to Chapter 4! In this chapter, we'll explore the power of embracing frugality as a means to minimize expenses and optimize your lifestyle. By adopting smart spending habits and making conscious choices, you can save more money, increase your savings rate, and accelerate your journey towards financial independence and early retirement.

4.1.1 Cutting Unnecessary Expenses

To effectively reduce your expenses, it's essential to identify and eliminate unnecessary spending. Here are some strategies to consider:

1. Track Your Expenses: Start by tracking your expenses to gain a clear understanding of where your money is going. Use budgeting apps, spreadsheets, or financial management tools to categorize and analyze your spending habits.
2. Analyze Your Budget: Review your budget and identify areas where you can cut back. Look for non-essential expenses such as dining out, subscriptions, entertainment, or impulse purchases that can be reduced or eliminated.
3. Prioritize Your Spending: Differentiate between needs and wants. Prioritize essential expenses like housing, food, utilities, and healthcare while minimizing discretionary spending on non-essential items.
4. Avoid Lifestyle Inflation: As your income increases, resist

the temptation to inflate your lifestyle and spend more. Instead, maintain or even decrease your expenses, allowing you to save and invest a larger portion of your income.

5. Negotiate Bills and Contracts: Take the time to negotiate bills and contracts for services such as internet, cable, insurance, or gym memberships. Often, service providers are willing to offer discounts or lower rates to retain customers.

By consciously evaluating and reducing unnecessary expenses, you can free up more money to save and invest, bringing you closer to financial independence.

4.1.2 Strategies for Smart Shopping and Saving

In addition to cutting unnecessary expenses, adopting smart shopping and saving strategies can further optimize your spending habits. Consider the following:

1. Create a Shopping List: Before going shopping, make a list of the items you need. Stick to your list and avoid impulse purchases that can derail your budget.
2. Compare Prices and Look for Discounts: Research prices online and compare deals from different retailers to ensure you're getting the best value for your money. Take advantage of coupons, promo codes, or loyalty programs to save even more.
3. Buy in Bulk: For items you regularly use, consider buying in bulk to take advantage of discounted prices. This approach can save you money in the long run, especially for non-perishable goods.

4. Embrace Secondhand and Thrift Shopping: Explore secondhand stores, thrift shops, or online platforms to find quality items at a fraction of the cost. This is particularly beneficial for clothing, furniture, books, and electronics.
5. Automate Savings: Set up automatic transfers from your paycheck or bank account to a separate savings or investment account. This way, you'll save consistently without relying on willpower.
6. Practice Delayed Gratification: Before making a non-essential purchase, give yourself some time to consider if it aligns with your long-term goals. Delaying gratification can help you make more mindful spending decisions and avoid impulsive purchases.

Remember, optimizing your expenses doesn't mean depriving yourself of all pleasures. It's about finding a balance and prioritizing your spending based on your values and long-term goals.

4.2 Housing and Transportation Optimization

Welcome to the section on housing and transportation optimization! In this section, we'll explore strategies for evaluating housing options, reducing housing costs, and finding efficient transportation solutions. By making informed choices in these areas, you can significantly impact your financial well-being and progress towards financial independence and early retirement.

4.2.1 Evaluating Housing Options and Reducing Housing Costs

Housing is often one of the largest expenses in our lives. By carefully evaluating your housing options and finding ways to reduce costs, you can free up more money for savings and investments. Consider the following strategies:

1. Determine Your Needs: Assess your housing needs realistically. Consider the size, location, and amenities required for your lifestyle. Avoid unnecessary space or features that can drive up costs.
2. Renting vs. Buying: Evaluate the pros and cons of renting versus buying a home. In some cases, renting may be more cost-effective, especially in areas with high real estate prices or if you value flexibility. Calculate the total cost of ownership, including mortgage payments, property taxes, insurance, and maintenance, to make an informed decision.
3. Location Considerations: Opt for a location that balances affordability with convenience. Look for areas with lower housing costs but still offer access to essential amenities, transportation options, and proximity to your work or preferred lifestyle activities.
4. House Hacking: Consider house hacking strategies to reduce housing costs. This can involve renting out a portion of your home, having roommates, or utilizing short-term rental platforms when you're away. These arrangements can help offset your housing expenses significantly.
5. Downsize or Refinance: If you currently own a home, assess whether downsizing or refinancing is a viable option. Smaller homes or refinancing to a lower interest rate can reduce mortgage payments and overall housing costs.

Remember, finding affordable housing doesn't mean sacrificing comfort or safety. It's about finding a balance that aligns with your financial goals and lifestyle preferences.

4.2.2 Efficient Transportation Solutions

Transportation costs can also have a significant impact on your overall expenses. By adopting efficient transportation solutions, you can save money and reduce your environmental footprint. Consider the following strategies:

1. Public Transportation: Utilize public transportation options such as buses, trains, or subways whenever possible. This can significantly reduce commuting costs, including fuel, parking, and vehicle maintenance expenses.
2. Carpooling and Ride-Sharing: Explore carpooling with colleagues, neighbors, or friends who share a similar commute. Alternatively, consider ride-sharing services to split transportation costs with others going in the same direction.
3. Active Transportation: Incorporate more active transportation methods into your routine, such as walking or cycling. Not only does this save on transportation costs, but it also promotes better health and well-being.
4. Evaluate Vehicle Ownership: Assess whether owning a vehicle is necessary. In some cases, relying on car-sharing services, renting, or using ride-sharing apps may be more cost-effective, especially if you have limited driving needs.
5. Efficient Vehicle Choices: If vehicle ownership is necessary, choose fuel-efficient models and consider electric or hybrid options. These vehicles typically have lower fuel and

maintenance costs, helping you save in the long run.

6. Maintenance and Fuel Efficiency: Regularly maintain your vehicle to ensure optimal fuel efficiency. Keep tires properly inflated, perform routine maintenance checks, and adopt fuel-efficient driving habits, such as avoiding aggressive acceleration or unnecessary idling.

By adopting efficient transportation solutions, you can save money, reduce your environmental impact, and potentially enjoy a more stress-free commute.

4.3 Balancing Frugality with Enjoying Life's Experiences

Welcome to the section on balancing frugality with enjoying life's experiences! While it's important to be mindful of your expenses, it's equally crucial to find a balance that allows you to enjoy life and create meaningful experiences. In this section, we'll explore strategies for prioritizing value-based spending and finding affordable ways to travel and entertain yourself.

4.3.1 Prioritizing Value-Based Spending

Value-based spending involves aligning your expenses with what truly matters to you. By focusing on the things that bring you joy and fulfillment, you can spend your money wisely and avoid wasteful spending. Consider the following strategies:

1. Identify Your Values: Reflect on what truly matters to you in life. What brings you happiness and satisfaction? It could be spending time with loved ones, pursuing hobbies, supporting causes you care about, or personal growth. Clarify your values to guide your spending decisions.

2. Conscious Consumption: Before making a purchase, ask yourself if it aligns with your values and contributes to your overall well-being. Avoid impulse buying and give yourself time to consider if the purchase will genuinely enhance your life.
3. Quality Over Quantity: Prioritize quality over quantity when making purchases. Invest in durable, long-lasting products or experiences that bring you lasting value, even if they may come with a higher upfront cost.
4. Experiences Over Material Possessions: Instead of accumulating material possessions, focus on creating memorable experiences. Plan activities, outings, and trips that align with your interests and values, as these experiences often provide greater long-term satisfaction.
5. Mindful Gifting: When giving gifts to others, focus on thoughtful and meaningful gestures rather than extravagant spending. Consider homemade gifts, experiences shared together, or contributions to causes the recipient cares about.

Remember, value-based spending doesn't mean completely depriving yourself of occasional indulgences. It's about consciously allocating your resources towards what truly matters and brings you lasting happiness.

4.3.2 Strategies for Affordable Travel and Entertainment

Travel and entertainment can be enriching experiences, but they often come with associated expenses. By adopting smart strategies, you can enjoy these activities without breaking the bank. Consider the following:

1. Travel Hacking: Explore travel hacking techniques such as accumulating rewards points, utilizing airline miles, or taking advantage of credit card perks. These strategies can help you save on flights, accommodation, and other travel expenses.
2. Off-Peak Travel: Plan your trips during off-peak seasons or weekdays when travel costs are typically lower. Research and compare prices to find the best deals on flights, accommodations, and attractions.
3. Alternative Accommodations: Consider alternative accommodations like vacation rentals, hostels, or house-sitting opportunities. These options often provide more affordable alternatives to traditional hotels while offering unique experiences.
4. Local Exploration: You don't always have to travel far to enjoy new experiences. Explore your local area and discover hidden gems, parks, museums, festivals, or cultural events. Engaging in local activities can be both affordable and rewarding.
5. Free and Low-Cost Entertainment: Take advantage of free or low-cost entertainment options such as community events, public parks, art exhibitions, concerts, or outdoor activities. Research your local area for budget-friendly entertainment opportunities.
6. Group Discounts and Coupons: Look for group discounts or coupons for attractions, entertainment venues, or dining establishments. Websites, apps, or membership programs often offer discounted rates that can significantly reduce your expenses.

Remember, the key is to find a balance between enjoying life's experiences and staying within your financial means. By being resourceful and seeking out affordable options, you can continue to create cherished memories without compromising your financial goals.

Chapter 5: Creating a Robust Investment Strategy

5.1 Understanding Different Investment Vehicles

Welcome to Chapter 5! In this chapter, we'll delve into the world of investing and explore different investment vehicles that can help you grow your wealth and achieve financial independence. By understanding the options available to you, you can create a robust investment strategy tailored to your goals and risk tolerance.

5.1.1 Stocks, Bonds, and Mutual Funds

Stocks, bonds, and mutual funds are among the most common investment vehicles. Each offers unique characteristics and potential returns. Let's take a closer look:

1. Stocks: Investing in individual stocks means becoming a partial owner of a company. Stocks offer the potential for high returns but also come with higher risk. Research and analyze individual companies before investing, considering factors such as their financial performance, industry trends, and competitive advantages.
2. Bonds: Bonds are debt instruments issued by governments, municipalities, or corporations. When you invest in bonds, you are essentially lending money to the issuer in exchange for regular interest payments and the return of the principal at maturity. Bonds are generally considered lower-risk investments compared to stocks, but they may offer lower returns.
3. Mutual Funds: Mutual funds pool money from multiple

investors to invest in a diversified portfolio of stocks, bonds, or other assets. By investing in a mutual fund, you gain exposure to a range of securities without needing to select individual investments. Mutual funds are managed by professional fund managers, and they offer diversification and convenience for investors.

When considering these investment options, it's important to assess your risk tolerance, investment goals, and time horizon. Diversification across different asset classes can help reduce risk and potentially increase your chances of achieving long-term growth.

5.1.2 Real Estate and Property Investment

Real estate and property investment can be an attractive avenue for wealth accumulation and diversification. Here are some key considerations:

1. Rental Properties: Owning rental properties can provide both regular rental income and potential appreciation of the property's value over time. However, it requires careful management, property maintenance, and understanding local rental market dynamics.
2. Real Estate Investment Trusts (REITs): REITs are companies that own, operate, or finance income-generating real estate. By investing in REITs, you can gain exposure to real estate assets without the need for direct property ownership. REITs are traded on stock exchanges and offer dividends to investors.
3. Real Estate Crowdfunding: Real estate crowdfunding platforms allow individuals to invest in real estate projects

or properties with smaller amounts of capital. These platforms bring together investors and property developers, providing access to real estate opportunities that may otherwise be inaccessible.

4. Real Estate Investment Groups: Real estate investment groups are formed by individuals pooling their resources to invest in properties collectively. This approach allows for shared costs, management responsibilities, and the potential for higher returns through collective expertise.

Before venturing into real estate investments, thoroughly research the local market, consider the associated costs (including property taxes, insurance, and maintenance), and evaluate the potential for rental income and property appreciation.

Remember, investing involves risks, and it's important to diversify your portfolio to spread out risk and align your investments with your financial goals and risk tolerance.

5.2 Diversifying Your Investment Portfolio

Welcome to the section on diversifying your investment portfolio! Diversification is a fundamental principle of sound investing, as it helps spread risk and enhances the potential for long-term growth. In this section, we'll explore asset allocation strategies and how to build a well-balanced investment portfolio.

5.2.1 Asset Allocation Strategies

Asset allocation is the process of dividing your investment portfolio among different asset classes, such as stocks, bonds, real estate, and cash equivalents. The goal is to achieve a mix that aligns with your financial goals, risk tolerance, and time horizon. Here are some common asset allocation strategies:

1. Risk Tolerance-Based Allocation: This strategy involves determining your risk tolerance and allocating assets accordingly. If you have a higher risk tolerance, you may allocate more to stocks for potential higher returns. Conversely, if you have a lower risk tolerance, you might lean towards a higher allocation in bonds and cash equivalents for stability.
2. Age-Based Allocation: With this approach, you consider your age and time remaining until retirement. Younger investors with more time to recover from market downturns may choose a more aggressive allocation with a higher percentage in stocks. As you approach retirement, a more conservative allocation may be favored to protect your wealth.
3. Target Date Funds: Target date funds are mutual funds designed to automatically adjust their asset allocation based on your target retirement date. These funds become more conservative as the target date approaches, easing risk as you near retirement.
4. Core-Satellite Allocation: In this approach, you create a "core" portfolio consisting of broad-market index funds or exchange-traded funds (ETFs) that represent the overall market. Then, you add "satellite" investments, such as individual stocks or sector-specific funds, to enhance returns or target specific opportunities.
5. Risk Parity Allocation: Risk parity aims to achieve an equal level of risk across different asset classes. It involves

allocating more to traditionally less volatile assets (like bonds) and less to riskier assets (like stocks) to achieve a balanced risk profile.

5.2.2 Building a Well-Balanced Portfolio

Building a well-balanced portfolio is about diversifying across different investments to minimize risk while pursuing growth. Consider the following steps:

1. Define Your Goals: Clarify your financial goals and investment time horizon. Short-term goals may favor more stable assets, while long-term goals may allow for greater exposure to growth-oriented assets.
2. Research Investments: Conduct thorough research on various investment options, considering historical performance, fees, management, and risk factors. Diversify across multiple industries, regions, and asset classes to avoid concentration risk.
3. Monitor and Rebalance: Regularly review your portfolio's performance and rebalance as needed to maintain your target asset allocation. Market fluctuations can cause imbalances, and rebalancing ensures your portfolio stays aligned with your risk tolerance and goals.
4. Consider Professional Advice: If you're unsure about your investment strategy or lack the time to manage your portfolio actively, consider seeking advice from a certified financial planner or investment advisor.

Remember, while diversification can reduce risk, it doesn't guarantee against losses. Be prepared for market fluctuations and focus on a long-term investment approach. A well-diversified portfolio can provide the foundation for achieving your financial independence and early retirement goals.

5.3 Minimizing Risk and Maximizing Returns

Welcome to the section on minimizing risk and maximizing returns! Investing involves balancing the potential for returns with the inherent risks. In this section, we'll explore the importance of investment research and due diligence, as well as long-term investing strategies to help you navigate the investment landscape effectively.

5.3.1 Investment Research and Due Diligence

Thorough investment research and due diligence are essential for making informed investment decisions. Here are some key considerations:

1. Fundamental Analysis: Conduct fundamental analysis to evaluate the financial health and performance of companies or assets. Consider factors such as earnings, revenue growth, debt levels, competitive positioning, and industry trends. This analysis can help you assess the intrinsic value of an investment.
2. Technical Analysis: Use technical analysis to analyze historical price and volume data, identify patterns, and make predictions about future price movements. Technical analysis can help inform entry and exit points for trades but should not be the sole basis for investment decisions.
3. Economic and Market Analysis: Stay informed about macroeconomic trends, industry-specific developments, and geopolitical events that may impact your investments.

Regularly review financial news, reports, and market analysis to gauge the overall market conditions and make well-informed decisions.

4. Risk Assessment: Evaluate the risks associated with your investments, including market risk, credit risk, liquidity risk, and geopolitical risk. Consider how these risks may affect your investment returns and make appropriate adjustments to your portfolio.
5. Due Diligence: Conduct thorough due diligence when evaluating investment opportunities, including analyzing financial statements, examining historical performance, understanding the management team, and assessing the competitive landscape. Seek independent opinions and consult professionals if needed.

Remember, investment research and due diligence are ongoing processes. Stay vigilant, continuously monitor your investments, and be prepared to make adjustments as new information becomes available.

5.3.2 Long-Term Investing Strategies

Long-term investing focuses on holding investments over an extended period to benefit from the power of compounding and ride out short-term market fluctuations. Consider the following strategies:

1. Dollar-Cost Averaging: Regularly invest a fixed amount of money into your portfolio, regardless of market conditions. This strategy reduces the impact of short-term market volatility and allows you to accumulate more shares

when prices are low.

2. Buy and Hold: Select high-quality investments and hold them for the long term. This approach avoids the temptation to time the market and focuses on the underlying value and potential growth of the investment over time.
3. Reinvest Dividends: If you receive dividends from your investments, reinvest them back into the portfolio. This practice accelerates the compounding effect, potentially increasing your returns over the long term.
4. Patience and Discipline: Successful long-term investing requires patience and discipline. Avoid making impulsive investment decisions based on short-term market movements. Stick to your investment strategy and maintain a long-term perspective.
5. Review and Adjust: Regularly review your investment portfolio and make adjustments as needed based on changes in your financial goals, risk tolerance, and market conditions. However, avoid making knee-jerk reactions to short-term market fluctuations.

By adopting a long-term investing mindset and combining it with diligent research and due diligence, you can mitigate risks and increase the potential for higher returns over time.

Chapter 6: Tax Optimization and Retirement Accounts

6.1 The Importance of Tax Planning

Welcome to Chapter 6! In this chapter, we'll explore the importance of tax planning and how it can help you optimize your finances on the path to financial independence and early retirement. Understanding the tax system and implementing strategies to minimize your tax liability can significantly impact your long-term financial success.

6.1.1 Maximizing Deductions and Tax Credits

One of the key aspects of tax planning is maximizing deductions and taking advantage of tax credits. Here are some strategies to consider:

1. Itemized Deductions: Evaluate whether itemizing deductions would be more beneficial than taking the standard deduction. Common itemized deductions include mortgage interest, property taxes, state and local taxes, charitable contributions, and certain medical expenses.
2. Retirement Contributions: Contribute to tax-advantaged retirement accounts, such as a 401(k), Individual Retirement Account (IRA), or a Self-Employed Retirement Plan (SEP IRA or Solo 401(k)). These contributions may be tax-deductible, helping reduce your taxable income and potentially lowering your tax liability.
3. Education Tax Benefits: Take advantage of education-related tax benefits, such as the Lifetime Learning Credit

or the American Opportunity Credit. These credits can offset the costs of higher education expenses for yourself, your spouse, or your dependents.

4. Health Savings Accounts (HSAs): If you have a high-deductible health plan, contribute to an HSA. Contributions are tax-deductible, and withdrawals used for qualified medical expenses are tax-free, making it a powerful tool for both saving on taxes and covering medical costs.
5. Tax Credits: Familiarize yourself with available tax credits, such as the Child Tax Credit, Earned Income Tax Credit, or the Saver's Credit. These credits directly reduce your tax liability and can result in significant savings.

It's important to consult with a tax professional or utilize tax software to ensure you're maximizing your deductions and credits within the confines of the tax laws.

6.1.2 Strategies for Tax-Efficient Investing

Tax-efficient investing aims to minimize the tax impact on your investment returns. Here are a few strategies to consider:

1. Asset Location: Allocate investments strategically between taxable and tax-advantaged accounts. Generally, tax-efficient investments, such as index funds or tax-efficient ETFs, are best held in taxable accounts, while tax-inefficient investments, like actively managed funds or bond funds, are better suited for tax-advantaged retirement accounts.
2. Tax-Loss Harvesting: Offset capital gains by strategically

selling investments at a loss. This strategy can help reduce your taxable income and potentially generate tax deductions.

3. Dividend Reinvestment: If you receive dividends from your investments, consider reinvesting them back into the same investment within a tax-advantaged account. By doing so, you can defer taxes on the dividends until you eventually sell the investment.
4. Long-Term Capital Gains: Hold investments for at least one year to qualify for the lower long-term capital gains tax rates. Short-term gains are typically taxed at your ordinary income tax rates, which are generally higher.
5. Roth Conversions: If you have a Traditional IRA or 401(k), consider converting a portion of the funds to a Roth IRA. While you'll pay taxes on the converted amount, future qualified withdrawals from the Roth IRA can be tax-free.

Remember that tax laws can change, so it's crucial to stay updated and consult with a tax advisor to ensure your investment strategies align with the current tax regulations.

6.2 Understanding Retirement Accounts

Welcome to the section on retirement accounts! Retirement accounts are powerful tools for building wealth and securing a comfortable retirement. In this section, we'll explore different types of retirement accounts and strategies for maximizing contributions and taking advantage of employer matches.

6.2.1 401(k), IRA, and Roth IRA Explained

There are several types of retirement accounts, each with its own rules and tax advantages. Here are the key features of three common retirement accounts:

1. 401(k): A 401(k) is an employer-sponsored retirement account. Contributions to a traditional 401(k) are made with pre-tax dollars, reducing your taxable income in the year of contribution. The funds grow tax-deferred, meaning you won't pay taxes until you withdraw them during retirement. Some employers also offer Roth 401(k) options, where contributions are made with after-tax dollars, but qualified withdrawals in retirement are tax-free.
2. Individual Retirement Account (IRA): An IRA is an individual retirement account that you can open on your own. Like a traditional 401(k), contributions to a traditional IRA are tax-deductible, and the funds grow tax-deferred. Roth IRAs, on the other hand, are funded with after-tax dollars, but qualified withdrawals in retirement are tax-free.
3. Roth IRA: A Roth IRA is an individual retirement account where contributions are made with after-tax dollars, allowing for tax-free growth and tax-free withdrawals in retirement, as long as certain conditions are met.

It's important to note that each type of retirement account has contribution limits and eligibility requirements based on your income and employment status. Additionally, there are penalties for early withdrawals before reaching the specified retirement age.

6.2.2 Maximizing Contributions and Employer Matches

Contributing to retirement accounts is a crucial step in building long-term wealth. Here are some strategies to consider for maximizing contributions and taking advantage of employer matches:

1. Maximize Employer Matches: If your employer offers a 401(k) match, contribute at least enough to receive the full match. Employer matches are essentially free money and can significantly boost your retirement savings.
2. Contribute Regularly: Make consistent contributions to your retirement accounts, whether through automatic payroll deductions or regular monthly contributions. This habit helps you build savings over time and take advantage of dollar-cost averaging.
3. Take Advantage of Catch-Up Contributions: If you're age 50 or older, you're eligible to make additional catch-up contributions to certain retirement accounts. Catch-up contributions allow you to accelerate your savings and make up for any gaps in your retirement planning.
4. Prioritize Roth Contributions: Depending on your financial situation and tax planning strategy, consider prioritizing Roth contributions. Roth accounts offer tax-free withdrawals in retirement, which can be advantageous if you expect to be in a higher tax bracket in the future.
5. Review and Adjust Contributions: Regularly review your retirement contributions and consider increasing them whenever possible. As your income grows or expenses decrease, allocate a portion of the additional funds towards retirement savings.

Remember, retirement contributions should align with your overall financial plan and goals. It's recommended to consult with a financial advisor or retirement specialist to determine the most suitable contribution strategy for your specific circumstances.

6.3 Planning for Early Retirement

Welcome to the section on planning for early retirement! Achieving financial independence and retiring early requires careful planning and consideration. In this section, we'll explore strategies for withdrawing retirement funds early and creating a sustainable retirement income stream that will support your desired lifestyle.

6.3.1 Strategies for Withdrawing Retirement Funds Early

Retiring early means you'll need to access your retirement funds before the traditional retirement age. Here are some strategies to consider for early retirement fund withdrawals:

1. Roth IRA Conversion Ladder: If you have funds in a traditional IRA or 401(k), you can utilize a Roth IRA Conversion Ladder. This involves converting a portion of your traditional retirement account funds into a Roth IRA each year, and after five years, you can withdraw the converted funds without penalty or tax. This strategy allows you to access your retirement savings early while minimizing taxes and penalties.
2. 72(t) Substantially Equal Periodic Payments (SEPP): Under the IRS Rule 72(t), you can take substantially equal periodic payments from your retirement account penalty-free if certain conditions are met. This strategy involves calculating and committing to a fixed withdrawal amount

based on your life expectancy or a specified period of time. It's essential to consult with a financial advisor or tax professional to ensure compliance with the IRS rules and avoid penalties.

3. Taxable Investment Accounts: If you have substantial investments in taxable accounts, you can use these funds to bridge the gap between early retirement and accessing your retirement accounts penalty-free. By strategically managing your taxable investments, you can create an income stream to support your living expenses.
4. Health Savings Account (HSA): If you have an HSA and are retiring early, you can use the funds for qualified medical expenses tax-free. After age 65, you can also withdraw funds for non-medical expenses penalty-free, though you'll owe income tax on the withdrawals.

Remember that early retirement fund withdrawals require careful planning to avoid penalties and ensure a sustainable retirement income stream. Consult with a financial advisor or retirement specialist to develop a customized strategy that aligns with your specific circumstances.

6.3.2 Creating a Sustainable Retirement Income Stream

When retiring early, it's essential to create a sustainable retirement income stream that will support your desired lifestyle for potentially several decades. Here are some strategies to consider:

1. Portfolio Withdrawal Strategies: Determine a safe withdrawal rate from your investment portfolio that balances your income needs with preserving the principal.

The 4% rule is a commonly cited guideline, suggesting that withdrawing 4% of your initial portfolio value annually, adjusted for inflation, provides a high probability of sustaining your funds over a 30-year retirement period. However, consider working with a financial advisor to customize the withdrawal rate based on your specific circumstances and risk tolerance.

2. Dividend Income: Focus on building a portfolio that generates reliable dividend income. Dividend-paying stocks and dividend-focused funds can provide a regular stream of income, supplementing your retirement funds.
3. Real Estate Investments: Consider real estate investments that generate rental income. Owning and managing rental properties can provide a consistent income stream in retirement.
4. Part-Time Work or Side Hustles: If you're comfortable with it, consider working part-time or pursuing side hustles in retirement. This can not only provide additional income but also help you stay engaged and fulfilled during your early retirement years.
5. Social Security Benefits: Depending on your age and work history, you may be eligible for Social Security benefits. However, it's important to evaluate the impact of early retirement on your benefit amount, as claiming benefits before full retirement age can result in reduced monthly payments.

Remember, creating a sustainable retirement income stream requires careful planning and ongoing monitoring of your financial situation. Regularly review and adjust your strategies to ensure your income remains sufficient to support your desired lifestyle throughout early retirement.

Conclusion:

Congratulations on completing this comprehensive guide to achieving financial independence and early retirement through the FIRE movement! Throughout this book, we have covered a wide range of topics, from understanding the FIRE mindset to mastering personal finance, maximizing income generation, minimizing expenses, and creating a robust investment strategy. By following the principles and strategies outlined in this book, you have laid a solid foundation for your financial future.

As you reflect on your FIRE journey, it's important to recognize the tremendous progress you have made. You have gained a deep understanding of personal finance, developed effective budgeting skills, managed debt, optimized credit, and learned about various investment options and strategies. You have explored alternative income sources, enhanced your career prospects, embraced frugality, and prioritized value-based spending. Additionally, you have gained insights into tax optimization, retirement accounts, and early withdrawal strategies. All of these accomplishments have brought you closer to the ultimate goal of financial independence and early retirement.

However, it's crucial to understand that achieving financial independence is not a one-time achievement but a lifelong commitment. Financial discipline and continuous learning will be key in maintaining and growing your wealth. The financial landscape and markets are constantly evolving, so staying informed and adapting to new opportunities and challenges is essential.

As you embark on this new chapter of financial independence, I encourage you to take action. Implement the strategies and techniques you have learned in this book and adapt them to your unique circumstances. Create a personalized financial plan, set goals, and regularly review your progress. Seek advice from professionals, engage in discussions with like-minded individuals, and stay motivated along the way.

Remember, financial independence is not just about accumulating wealth. It's about having the freedom and flexibility to live life on your own terms, pursuing your passions, and enjoying meaningful experiences. As you navigate this journey, be intentional about aligning your financial decisions with your values and aspirations.

I wish you all the success and fulfillment in your pursuit of financial freedom. May you continue to grow, learn, and inspire others with your FIRE journey. The path to financial independence is within your reach, so seize the opportunity and create the life you desire. Here's to a future filled with abundance, contentment, and the joy of early retirement!

Appendix:

1. Additional Resources and Books:

- "Your Money or Your Life" by Vicki Robin and Joe Dominguez
- "The Simple Path to Wealth" by JL Collins
- "Bogleheads' Guide to Investing" by Taylor Larimore, Mel Lindauer, and Michael LeBoeuf
- "Choose FI: Your Blueprint to Financial Independence" by Chris Mamula, Brad Barrett, and Jonathan Mendonsa
- "The Millionaire Next Door" by Thomas J. Stanley and William D. Danko
- "Early Retirement Extreme" by Jacob Lund Fisker

1. Websites and Online Communities:

- Financial Independence subreddit (r/financialindependence)
- ChooseFI (https://www.choosefi.com[1])
- Mr. Money Mustache (https://www.mrmoneymustache.com[2])
- Mad Fientist (https://www.madfientist.com[3])
- Bogleheads (https://www.bogleheads.org[4])

---

1. https://www.choosefi.com/

2. https://www.mrmoneymustache.com/

3. https://www.madfientist.com/

4. https://www.bogleheads.org/

1. Worksheets and Templates:

- Budgeting Worksheet: A template to track your income, expenses, and savings goals on a monthly basis.
- Net Worth Tracker: A tool to calculate and monitor your net worth over time, helping you assess your financial progress.
- Goal-Setting Worksheet: A guide to setting SMART (Specific, Measurable, Achievable, Relevant, Time-bound) goals and creating an action plan to achieve them.
- Investment Portfolio Tracker: A spreadsheet to monitor the performance and allocation of your investment portfolio.

1. Glossary of Key Financial Terms and Concepts:
    - A comprehensive glossary of financial terms and concepts, providing definitions and explanations to enhance your understanding of financial language and principles.

These additional resources, worksheets, and the glossary will serve as valuable companions to the knowledge and guidance provided in this book. Use them to deepen your understanding, refine your financial strategies, and stay on track towards achieving your financial goals.

Remember, financial independence and early retirement require dedication, discipline, and ongoing learning. Continuously educate yourself, seek advice from trusted sources, and surround yourself with a supportive community of like-minded individuals.

Best of luck on your continued journey towards financial independence and early retirement. May you achieve your goals and create a life of abundance, freedom, and fulfillment!

Don't miss out!

Visit the website below and you can sign up to receive emails whenever Alex Thompson publishes a new book. There's no charge and no obligation.

https://books2read.com/r/B-A-FEPY-HXGLC

BOOKS 2 READ

Connecting independent readers to independent writers.

Also by Alex Thompson

Alex on Finance
Financial Freedom Roadmap - Achieving Early Retirement through the FIRE Movement

Standalone
Side Hustle Success: Unlocking Your Entrepreneurial Potential
Side Hustle Success: The Ultimate Guide to Passive and Financial Freedom
Mastering the Markets: Advanced Trading Strategies for Success and Ethical Trading Practices
Financial Fortitude

www.ingramcontent.com/pod-product-compliance
Lightning Source LLC
LaVergne TN
LVHW090431210926
848480LV00002B/779